DISCOVER
AMERICA

NEW YORK

Val Lawton

AV² provides enriched content that supplements and complements this book. Weigl's AV² books strive to create inspired learning and engage young minds in a total learning experience.

Your AV² Media Enhanced books come alive with...

Audio
Listen to sections of the book read aloud.

Key Words
Study vocabulary, and complete a matching word activity.

Video
Watch informative video clips.

Quizzes
Test your knowledge.

Embedded Weblinks
Gain additional information for research.

Slide Show
View images and captions, and prepare a presentation.

Try This!
Complete activities and hands-on experiments.

... and much, much more!

Go to **www.av2books.com,** and enter this book's unique code.

BOOK CODE

Z 7 7 8 7 3 2

AV² by Weigl brings you media enhanced books that support active learning.

Published by AV² by Weigl
350 5th Avenue, 59th Floor
New York, NY 10118
Website: www.av2books.com

Library of Congress Cataloging-in-Publication Data
Names: Lawton, Val, author.
Title: New York : the empire state / Val Lawton.
Description: New York, NY : AV2 by Weigl, 2016. | Series: Discover America |
  Includes index.
Identifiers: LCCN 2015048031 (print) | LCCN 2015049099 (ebook) | ISBN
  9781489649119 (hard cover : alk. paper) | ISBN 9781489649126 (soft cover :
  alk. paper) | ISBN 9781489649133 (Multi-User eBook)
Subjects: LCSH: New York (State)--Juvenile literature.
Classification: LCC F119.3 .L392 2016 (print) | LCC F119.3 (ebook) | DDC 974.7--dc23
LC record available at http://lccn.loc.gov/2015048031

Printed in the United States of America, in Brainerd, Minnesota
1 2 3 4 5 6 7 8 9 20 19 18 17 16

052016
270516

Project Coordinator Heather Kissock
Art Director Terry Paulhus

NEW YORK

Contents

STATE TREE
Sugar Maple

STATE BIRD
Eastern Bluebird

STATE ANIMAL
Beaver

STATE FLAG
New York

STATE FLOWER
Rose

STATE SEAL
New York

Nickname
The Empire State

Motto
Excelsior
(Ever Upward)

Song
"I Love New York," words and
music by Steve Karmen

Population
(2014 Census) 19,746,227
Ranked 3rd state

Entered the Union
July 26, 1788, as the 11th state

Capital
Albany

Discover New York

Few places in the United States can rival New York State's population, economic power, and cultural importance. The value of goods and services produced in the state is higher than that of most countries. From its sandy beaches and rugged mountains to the hustle and bustle of New York City, the state of New York is a place of sharp contrasts.

New York was one of the original 13 colonies. Its nickname, the Empire State, is thought to have come from George Washington, who called New York the "seat of empire." The people of New York have worked hard to live up to their state's nickname. Today, New York is a national leader in manufacturing, finance, education, and the arts.

New York is part of the Middle Atlantic region of the United States. From southwest to northeast, New York is bordered by Lake Erie, the Canadian province of Ontario, Lake Ontario, and the Canadian province of Quebec. To the east are the New England states of Vermont, Massachusetts, and Connecticut. The Atlantic Ocean and New Jersey are to the southeast, and Pennsylvania is to the south.

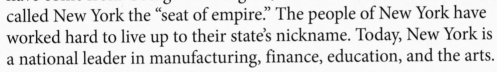

New York suffered a devastating loss on September 11, 2001, when terrorists flew two jet aircraft into the 110-story twin towers of the World Trade Center. The towers burned and collapsed, killing some 2,800 people in New York City. Today, part of the area where the twin towers once stood has been turned into a memorial and museum. A new building, One World Trade Center, has also been erected in the space. It is the tallest skyscraper in the western hemisphere and was completed in 2013.

The Land

The Erie Canal was completed in 1825. It connects the Atlantic Ocean with the Great Lakes.

In 1789, New York City's **Federal Hall** was the site of **George Washington's inauguration** as the country's first president.

The **Staten Island Ferry** carries **20 million people** per year on a scenic 5-mile journey between Staten Island and lower Manhattan.

In the 1800s, the Hudson River Valley was nicknamed "Rhineland," because it reminded European settlers of the Rhine River Valley of Germany.

Beginnings

Two major Native American groups lived in the New York area starting in the 1300s. The Iroquois lived in the northern and central parts of the state, while the Algonquins lived in the south, in the area now called the Hudson River Valley.

The first Europeans arrived in the area in the seventeenth century. New Netherland, the first permanent colony, was established by the Dutch West India Company in 1624. New York City's Wall Street takes its name from a wall that was built by the Dutch in the seventeenth century to protect the city of New Amsterdam.

Fertile soil attracted settlers to the Hudson River Valley in the New Netherland colony. The British took control of New Netherland in 1664. The state of New York signed the Declaration of Independence, breaking from Great Britain, in 1776.

A key event in the history of the Empire State was the completion of the Erie Canal in 1825. It connected New York City with the Great Lakes via the Hudson River. The canal produced great revenues for the state and sped up development of the American frontier. In 1918, the New York State Barge Canal was opened to replace the Erie Canal. This system, now known as the New York State Canal System, incorporates parts of the Erie Canal and supports much water traffic.

Where is
NEW YORK?

Lake Huron

CANADA

Lake Ontario

The state of New York covers a total area of 54,556 square miles, making it the 27th largest state in the country. Land accounts for 47,214 square miles of New York's territory, with water making up the remaining 7,342 square miles. Parts of two of the Great Lakes, Ontario and Erie, account for more than half of the water area.

United States Map

Alaska   Hawai'i

New York

Lake Erie

MAP LEGEND

- ■ New York
- ☆ Capital City
- ● Major City
- ▲ Letchworth State Park
- ◆ Thousand Islands
- ☐ Bordering States
- ☐ Canada
- ☐ Water

N

SCALE   0   50 miles

1 Albany

Located along the Hudson River, about 150 miles north of New York City, Albany was settled by the Dutch in 1624. It has been the capital of New York State since 1797. The city covers 21 square miles and has a population of about 94,000.

2 Letchworth State Park

Steep cliff walls line the gorge of Letchworth State Park. Forest thrives across the landscape. The Genesee River creates three sets of dramatic waterfalls, dropping up to 600 feet. Many people choose to visit in the fall to watch the leaves change color on the trees.

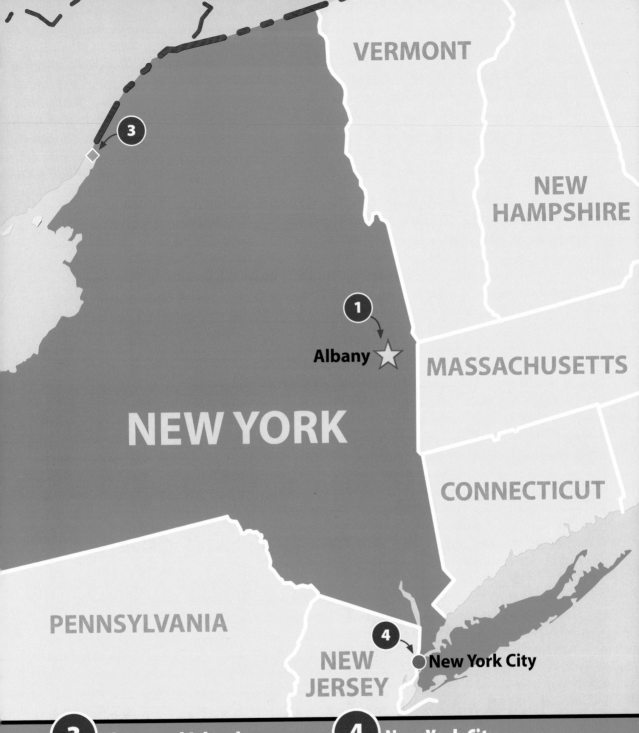

VERMONT

NEW HAMPSHIRE

MASSACHUSETTS

CONNECTICUT

PENNSYLVANIA

NEW JERSEY

NEW YORK

Albany

New York City

3 Thousand Islands

Thousand Islands encompasses more than a 50-mile stretch of the Saint Lawrence River. The islands extend over a granite shelf from the **Canadian Shield** to the Adirondack Mountains. Visitors can take a cruise to see the maze of islands. Numerous islands contain historic homes, ranging from log cabins to castles.

4 New York City

New York City is the ninth most populous city in the world and the state's largest city, with more than 8.4 million residents. The city is home to iconic streets such as Broadway, Wall Street, and the tourist area of Times Square. Visitors to the city can enjoy Central Park, located in Manhattan. The park is 3.5 square miles and has 37.5 million visitors per year.

Land Features

The landscape of New York State is varied. The largest natural region is the Appalachian Mountains, which cover about half of the state. The Appalachian region extends westward from the Hudson River valley to the state's southern and western boundaries. Within this area are the Catskill Mountains and the long, narrow bodies of water known as the Finger Lakes.

A lowland region runs northward along the Hudson River to Albany and then westward along the Mohawk River. A plateau-like region lies to the north of the Appalachian Mountains and west of the Mohawk River valley. It extends along the southern shores of the Great Lakes. The Adirondack Mountains lie east of this region.

Taughannock Falls

Taughannock Falls, in the Finger Lakes region, is the highest waterfall in New York State.

Hudson River

The Hudson River begins in northeastern New York, in the Adirondack Mountains. It then flows southward for more than 300 miles before emptying into New York Bay.

Finger Lakes

Canadice Lake, one of the 11 Finger Lakes, is a primary source of drinking water for the city of Rochester.

Mount Marcy

The state's tallest peak, Mount Marcy, stands 5,344 feet high and is located in the Adirondacks.

Climate

New York State generally has warm summers and cold winters. The coldest part of the state is in the Champlain Valley. In midtown Manhattan, temperatures average 32.1° Fahrenheit in January and 76.5°F in July. The area around Buffalo receives heavy snowfall. Much of Buffalo's frozen precipitation is "lake effect" snow, which occurs when cold winds blow over the warmer waters of Lake Erie.

Average Annual Precipitation Across New York

The amount of rainfall that different areas of New York typically receive each year can vary. What aspects of the geography of New York do you think contribute to this variation?

LEGEND

Average Annual Precipitation (in inches) 1961–1990

200 – 100.1

100 – 25.1

25 – 5 and less

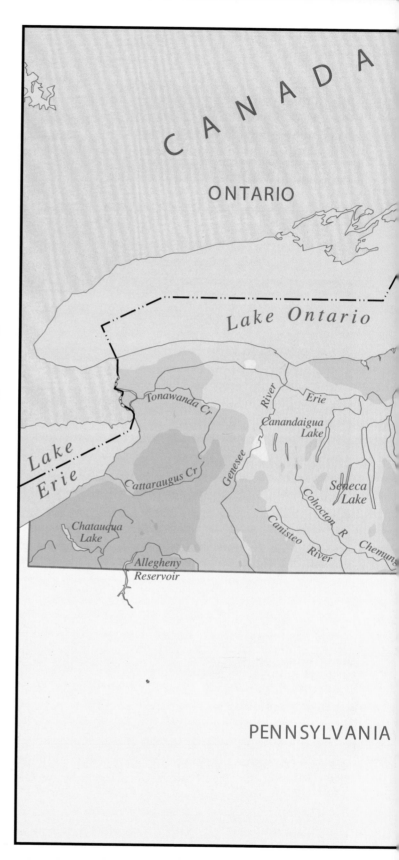

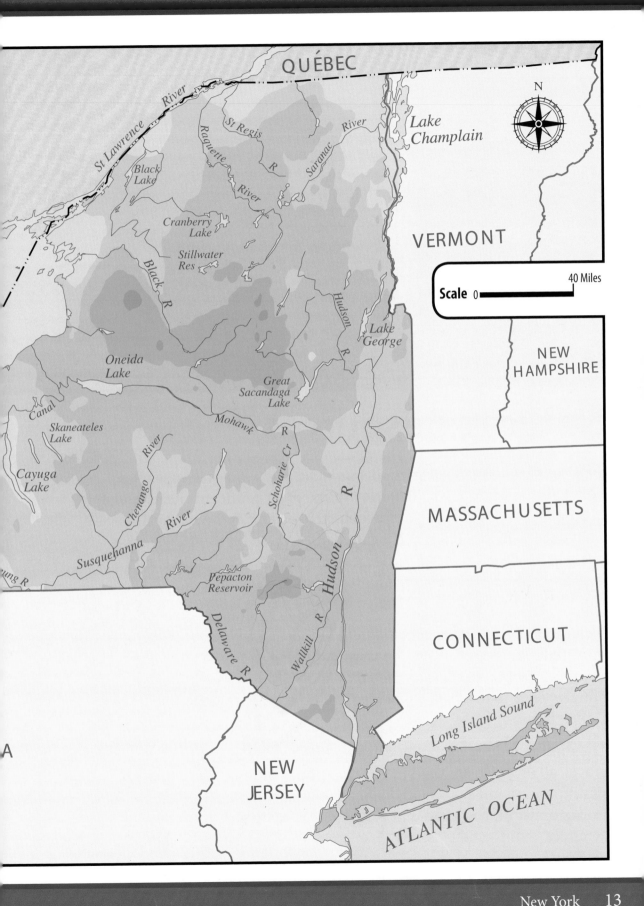

QUÉBEC

N

St Lawrence River

Raquette River

St Regis R

Saranac River

Lake Champlain

Black Lake

Cranberry Lake

Stillwater Res

Black R

Hudson R

Lake George

VERMONT

Scale 0   40 Miles

NEW HAMPSHIRE

Oneida Lake

Great Sacandaga Lake

Canal

Skaneateles Lake

River

Chenango

Mohawk R

Schoharie Cr

R

Cayuga Lake

River

MASSACHUSETTS

Susquehanna

Pepacton Reservoir

ung R

Delaware R

Wallkill R

Hudson R

CONNECTICUT

Long Island Sound

A

NEW JERSEY

ATLANTIC OCEAN

The water from the Niagara River and Falls is the biggest electricity producer in New York State. It generates enough power to light 24 million 100-watt bulbs at once.

Nature's Resources

One of New York's most important natural resources is water. The state has more than 8,000 lakes and many significant rivers. Some of New York's rivers provide **hydroelectric power** for homes and industry. In fact, the dam at Niagara Falls, located on the New York–Canadian border, is one of the largest producers of hydroelectricity in the world. The state also has a growing number of projects that use wind to produce electric power.

The state's inland and offshore waters support a commercial fishing industry. Major catches include clams, lobsters, squid, whiting, and flounder. People across the state enjoy pier fishing. One of the most popular piers to fish from is located just off the boardwalk on Coney Island.

The mining industry supplies crushed stone, cement, sand, and gravel, all of which are used in construction. The state also produces significant amounts of salt and zinc. The country's only major wollastonite mine is located in New York. Wollastonite is used in ceramics, paints, and plastics.

Wollastonite is mined in the Adirondack Mountains and in the Gouveneur District, in Lewis County.

Maple Ridge Wind Farm, located in upstate New York, is the largest wind farm in the state, with 195 turbines.

Vegetation

New York State was once almost entirely forested. As people settled the area, they cleared some of the forestland for farms or to build cities and towns. Today, forests cover more than half of New York's land area, and they feature a rich mixture of **deciduous** and **coniferous** species. Some 150 kinds of trees grow in the state. Among the softwoods found in New York's forests are white pines, spruces, and hemlocks. Hardwood trees include beeches, oaks, and yellow birches.

The sugar maple grows in many parts of the state. This particular maple produces sap that is tapped, collected, and boiled to make delicious maple syrup. In autumn, the leaves become bright red.

Many wild plants and flowers also grow throughout New York. Nearly 2,000 species of plants are native to the state. Flowering plants found in New York's forests include violets, bellworts, and hepaticas. In the spring, wildflowers such as buttercups, daisies, and asters decorate the state's meadows and hillsides.

Sugar Maples

Sugar maples thrive in cool, moist climates and grow to heights of 40 to 80 feet.

Lilac

Known for its lovely, long-lasting fragrance, the lilac is the official state bush.

Bellworts

The large-flowered bellwort is a woodland wildflower that blooms between mid-April and mid-May.

Pink Lady's Slipper

A member of the orchid family, the pink lady's slipper is found in a wide variety of New York habitats.

Wildlife

New York is home to a large variety of wildlife. Small mammals are common, such as the deer mouse, eastern cottontail rabbit, snowshoe hare, woodchuck, gray squirrel, muskrat, and raccoon. Larger mammals include the white-tailed deer, beaver, and black bear. Many mammals such as the cougar and gray wolf have been subject to overhunting, and are no longer found in nature in the state. Various wildlife management programs work to protect or reestablish certain animal populations. The state is home to many types of birds. The common house sparrow was introduced to the New York City area from Europe in the early 1850s.

New York's waters host an abundance of aquatic life. Many different species of freshwater fish are found in the state's lakes and rivers. These fish include bass, perch, pickerel, and trout. In the ocean, tuna, bass, flounder, and different kinds of shellfish can be found. The state's coastal waters also provide habitat for whales, dolphins, and seals.

Snowshoe Hare

Brown in summer, the snowshoe hare's coat turns white in winter, providing camouflage from predators.

Raccoon

Raccoons thrive in a wide variety of habitats throughout New York State.

House Sparrow

Abundant in New York, the common house sparrow usually makes its home in cities, suburbs, and towns, as well as other human settlements.

Dolphin

Dolphins, found in the Atlantic Ocean and Long Island Sound, are protected by federal law.

Economy

Times Square

Dozens of theaters, restaurants, and other attractions cluster around Times Square, in the heart of New York City.

Tourism

Each year, more than 45 million tourists visit New York City. Of these visitors, nearly 37 million come from the United States, and more than 8 million come from other countries. Tourists also enjoy the vast wilderness of the Adirondacks, the beaches of Long Island, and Chautauqua County's excellent birdwatching opportunities.

One of the state's greatest tourist draws is the world-renowned Niagara Falls. On the New York side, the falls are called the American Falls, and they cascade from a height of about 180 feet. Visitors can travel beneath the falls aboard the Maid of the Mist, a steamboat service that has been in operation since 1846.

Maid of the Mist

Since the mid-1800s, 11 Niagara Falls tour boats have carried the name Maid of the Mist. Four are still in service.

Central Park

Attracting about 25 million people annually, New York City's Central Park is the nation's most visited urban park.

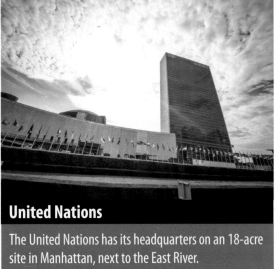

United Nations

The United Nations has its headquarters on an 18-acre site in Manhattan, next to the East River.

Manufacturing adds about $70 billion to the state economy each year. Chemical products make up the largest share, at $17 billion.

Primary Industries

New York is a major manufacturing center with more than 18,000 factories. These factories produce such items as electrical and medical equipment, computer equipment, clothing, plastics, chemicals, and **pharmaceuticals**. Many leading U.S. companies have their headquarters in New York City. The city is also a center of the media and entertainment industry. Many films and television programs are made in New York City's studios or use the city as a background.

Agriculture is important to New York's economy. Dairy farming is particularly significant. The state ranks second to Vermont in maple syrup production. Floriculture, the growing of decorative plants, also contributes to the economy.

New York has the **third-largest economy** of any state in the U.S., after California and Texas.

More than **53 million** passengers traveled through **John F. Kennedy** International **Airport in 2014.**

Value of Goods and Services
(in Millions of Dollars)

Besides manufacturing, the finance, media, and tourism industries are very important to the state's economy. What categories in the pie chart reflect the importance of tourism?

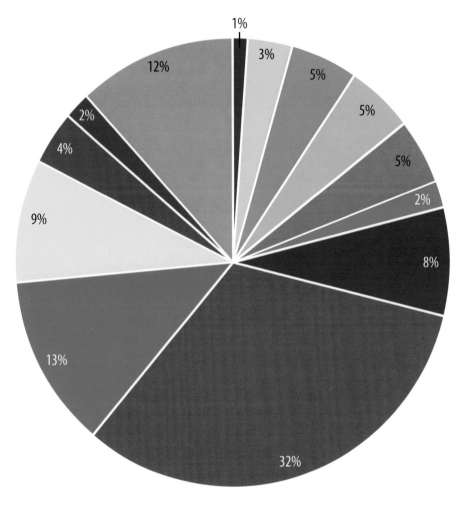

Agriculture, Forestry, Fishing, and Mining $4,442*

● Utilities $19,205

○ Construction $43,723

● Manufacturing $69,262

○ Wholesale Trade $70,767

● Retail Trade $65,752

● Transportation and Warehousing $25,847

● Information $108,329

● Finance, Insurance, and Real Estate $449,705

● Professional and Business Services $174,678

○ Education and Health Care $121,485

● Entertainment and Accommodations $54,055

● Other $27,438

○ Government $160,801

*Less than 1%

The New York Stock Exchange is the world's largest stock exchange in regard to how many trades are made daily. There are nearly 1 billion trades made there every day.

Goods and Services

New York provides the nation with a variety of goods, from fresh fruit to fashionable clothing to state-of-the-art electronic equipment. Many of New York's goods are exported to other states and countries. The state's excellent transportation system makes it a leader in distribution. Busy port facilities in places such as the New York City **metropolitan area**, Buffalo, and Albany handle many of these goods.

New York is the center of commerce and finance in the United States. The city's financial district, which is centered on Manhattan's Wall Street, is home to some of the world's most powerful banks, brokerage firms, and stock exchanges. The New York Stock Exchange is a driving force in the nation's economy. The exchange evolved from a meeting in 1792, when 24 New York City stockbrokers and merchants came together for trading purposes. Formally opened in 1817 as the New York Stock and Exchange Board, it remains one of the world's largest and most influential securities markets. NASDAQ, also headquartered in New York City, is another stock exchange with worldwide influence.

The State University of New York, created in 1948, is one of the world's largest educational organizations. Its many state-supported institutions of higher learning include major university centers at Stony Brook, Albany, Binghamton, and Buffalo. Many colleges that receive both state and local funds belong to a system known as the City University of New York.

New York's best-known private schools for higher education include Columbia University and the Juilliard School of Music, both in New York City, and Cornell University in Ithaca. The federal government operates the U.S. Military Academy at West Point and the U.S. Merchant Marine Academy at Kings Point on Long Island.

The first graduating class of West Point consisted of only 2 people in 1802. In 2015, nearly 1,000 graduated.

Many famous writers and artists have used the New York Public Library to create great works, including Betty Friedan, Francis Ford Coppola, and William Roy DeWitt Wallace, the creator of *Reader's Digest*.

Hendrick Theyanoguin was a Mohawk leader. During the early to mid 1700s, he was an ally to the British against the French expansion into what would later become the United States.

Longhouses were long buildings made up of a single room. Some longhouses were as long as 300 feet.

Native Americans

Archaeological evidence suggests that more than 8,000 early Native Americans lived in the New York area at one time. The earliest evidence of native groups is thought to be about 10,000 years ago. These early people lived along the banks of the lower Hudson River and on Staten, Long, and Manhattan Islands.

By the late 1500s, two major Native American groups, the Algonquian-speaking people and the Iroquois Confederacy, inhabited much of New York. The Algonquian people included the Mahican, or Mohican, and the Munsee. These groups lived chiefly in the Hudson Valley and on Long Island. Algonquian groups built and lived in long wooden structures called longhouses. These structures were often home to more than 50 people.

The Iroquois Confederacy, formed in 1570, originally included the Mohawk, the Oneida, the Onondaga, the Cayuga, and the Seneca. Like the Algonquian people, the Iroquois established farming communities and lived in longhouses. Each Iroquois community had a ruling council and a village chief, while the entire Iroquois Confederacy was run by a council of delegates.

Exploring the Land

The first European to visit the New York area is thought to be an Italian navigator, Giovanni da Verrazzano. Hired by the king of France to explore North America, Verrazzano sailed into New York Harbor in 1524. He left, however, without exploring the region.

Timeline of Settlement

First Colonies Established

1614 The Dutch build Fort Nassau near the site of present-day Albany. It is washed out by a flood.

1625 The Dutch settlement of New Amsterdam is founded at the southern end of Manhattan island.

1609 Samuel de Champlain explores the area of northeastern New York, and Henry Hudson explores the Hudson River region.

1626 Peter Minuit, the Dutch colonial governor, purchases Manhattan from the Lenape, a Native American group .

1524 Giovanni da Verrazzano enters New York Harbor.

1664 The British take control of the Dutch colony of New Netherland and rename it New York.

Early Exploration

In 1609, the French explorer Samuel de Champlain reached the lake that was later named after him. That same year, Henry Hudson, a British explorer, sailed up what was later named the Hudson River and claimed the land for the Netherlands. Employed by the Dutch East India Company, Hudson was assigned to find the Northwest Passage. This was a water route that was thought to exist and that would provide a shortcut to Asia.

Although Hudson did not find such a route, he wrote a report describing the New York area. This report generated interest from his employers in the Netherlands, and soon the Dutch claimed much of the New York region. The Dutch named the area New Netherland and began building permanent settlements.

1777 U.S. forces defeat the British in the Battle of Saratoga, an important victory that helped them win their independence several years later.

Territory and Statehood

1788 New York ratifies the Constitution and joins the Union as a state.

1776 British forces drive General George Washington's army out of the New York City area. The British occupy the city for the rest of the war.

1789 President George Washington is inaugurated in New York City, the first capital of the United States.

1776 As one of the original 13 colonies, New York signs the Declaration of Independence and joins the fight for freedom from British rule.

1825 The Erie Canal is completed.

1861–1865 Although the state sides with the Union during the Civil War, some New Yorkers riot against the military draft.

American Revolution

A large Huguenot group settled in Dover, New York, in the late 1600s.

The First Settlers

Most of the first permanent European settlers in New Netherland were French Huguenots. They were Protestants who had fled religious **persecution** in France. The Huguenots established Fort Orange in the northern Hudson Valley, at present-day Albany.

In 1625, the Dutch expanded their New Netherland colony with the founding of the city of New Amsterdam, on the southern tip of Manhattan Island. The New Netherland settlements grew slowly at first. To spur immigration, the Dutch West India Company offered large tracts of cheap land in 1629 to anyone who would bring 50 settlers to the colony within four years. Such people, known as patroons, became owners of vast amounts of land. They then rented plots of farmland to tenants. Unlike other colonies in North America, New Netherland tolerated all nationalities and religions. As a result, people from many different groups moved there.

When the British took control of New Netherland in 1664, the colony was renamed New York in honor of the duke of York. The colony grew rapidly between 1700 and the beginning of the American Revolutionary War in 1775, reaching a population of more than 160,000.

Peter Stuyvesant was the last Dutch governor of the New Netherland before the area was taken over by the British in 1664.

In 1674, the Treaty of Westminster ended the ongoing war between the Netherlands and England, and gave New Netherland to the English. Dutch Director-General Peter Stuyvesant led his troops out of New Netherland that same year.

History Makers

Two of the nation's most celebrated presidents were born in New York. The state has also been home to African American leaders, medical pioneers, and influential and extremely successful leaders in business and entertainment. Famous women, heroes, great explorers, and other famous Americans have also made New York their home.

Sojourner Truth (c. 1797–1883)

Born into slavery at a time when it was legal in New York State, Sojourner Truth escaped to freedom in 1826. She spent much of her adult life traveling from town to town, campaigning against slavery and for women's rights. A gifted preacher and singer, she also worked in Washington, D.C., during and after the Civil War to help slaves freed from the South.

Theodore Roosevelt (1858–1919)

A native of New York City, Theodore Roosevelt became a military hero during the Spanish-American War. He served as governor of New York and was elected U.S. vice president in 1898. He became president after William McKinley was shot to death in 1901. "TR" helped to preserve the nation's forests and wilderness areas, and he fought to limit the power of big corporations.

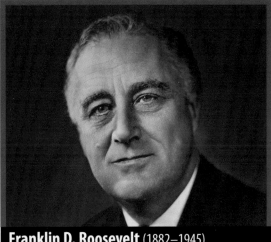

Franklin D. Roosevelt (1882–1945)

Born in Hyde Park, Franklin Roosevelt was stricken with polio in 1921 but fought back to overcome his disability. Like his distant cousin Theodore Roosevelt, "FDR" became governor of New York and U.S. president. Elected to a record four terms, he guided the country through the Great Depression of the 1930s and World War II.

Jonas Salk (1941–1995)

Born to Russian-Jewish immigrants in New York City, Jonas Salk was the first member of his family to attend college and become a doctor. In the 1940s and 1950s, he developed a vaccine against polio, a disease that had killed or crippled many thousands of children. He spent the rest of his life working on ways to protect people against other diseases.

Elena Kagan (1960–)

Elena Kagan was born in New York City in 1960. Her father was a lawyer, and her mother was a schoolteacher. Kagan eventually attended Princeton, Oxford, and Harvard, where she graduated with a law degree. In 2009, she was nominated by President Barack Obama to be the Solicitor General, becoming the first woman to hold that position in the United States. Kagan was also elected to the Supreme Court in 2010.

Culture

Manhattan is the most densely populated U.S. county, with more than 70,000 people per square mile.

In 2016, more than 55,000 students were enrolled at New York University.

The People Today

Millions of people, representing every ethnic group, entered the country through immigration stations at Castle Garden and Ellis Island in the 1800s and early 1900s, and many chose to stay in the state. New York is home to more than 19.3 million people and is one of the most densely populated states in the country. Compared to the national average of about 87 people per square mile of land area, New York State has about 410 people per square mile.

More than 40 percent of all state residents live in one of the five boroughs of New York City. The five boroughs are Manhattan, Brooklyn, the Bronx, Queens, and Staten Island. Many people who live in the outer boroughs and surrounding suburbs travel to work in Manhattan by subway, bus, commuter train, or car. Other leading population centers in the state include Buffalo, Rochester, Yonkers, Syracuse, and Albany, the state capital.

Between **2000** and **2010**, the population of New York only **increased** by **175,000** people.

Q What factors may cause such low population growth?

The largest room in the New York capitol building is the assembly chamber. Every year, about 2,000 bills and resolutions are voted on in the assembly chamber.

State Government

New York's first constitution was adopted in 1777. Under this constitution, George Clinton became the state's first governor to be directly elected by the people. New York's current constitution was adopted in 1894 and extensively revised in 1938. It has been amended many times.

The state government is divided into executive, legislative, and judicial branches. The governor heads the executive branch and serves a term of four years. The governor is responsible for proposing the state budget, appointing state department directors, and signing bills into law.

New York's legislative branch makes the laws. The state legislature has two parts, or chambers. There is a 62-member Senate and a 150-member Assembly. Senators and assembly members serve two-year terms. The judicial branch interprets and enforces the state's laws.

The Democratic Party has long been a powerful force in New York City politics. One of the most popular political leaders in recent New York State history was Mario Cuomo, a Democrat who served three four-year terms as governor, from 1983 through 1994. His son, Andrew Cuomo, was elected governor in November 2010.

The capitol building in Albany was built between 1867 and 1899.

Andrew Cuomo became the 56th governor of New York when he assumed office on January 1st, 2011.

New York's state song is
"O, Fair New York."

I LOVE NEW YORK
[repeat three times]
There isn't another like it
No matter where you go
And nobody can compare it
It's win and place and show
New York is special
New York is diff'rent
'Cause there's no place
else on earth
Quite like New York
And that's why
I LOVE NEW YORK
[repeat three times]

* excerpted

The New York City St. Patrick's Day Parade is the oldest and longest St. Patrick's Day parade in the world.

Celebrating Culture

Throughout the state's history, immigrants from many different countries have chosen to make their home in New York. The earliest European settlers came from the Netherlands, Great Britain, and Germany. Throughout the 1700s, 1800s, and early 1900s, the largest groups of immigrants arriving in New York came from Russia, Poland, Ireland, Austria, Canada, and England. Italy, Germany, and Romania also provided large numbers of newcomers.

Later in the twentieth century and in the early twenty-first century, immigrants came in great numbers from Africa, Asia, Central and South America, and the Caribbean islands. Immigration has made New York City the most culturally diverse city in the United States. The city's diversity can be seen in neighborhoods throughout the boroughs, including popular tourism destinations such as Little Italy and Chinatown.

Today, New York's largest minority groups are Hispanics and African Americans. In the Bronx, Latinos make up more than half the total population. People of Asian ancestry make up a growing share of the population of New York City.

New York State is home to more than 80,000 Native Americans. Many are descendants of the Six Nations of the Iroquois Confederacy. The Seneca and Mohawk are the largest of these groups. Three Seneca **reservations** are located in western New York, and the Mohawk have land in the northern part of the state. The Oneida Nation is also part of the Iroquois Confederacy. Today, people of the Oneida Nation live in central New York.

The Great Mohican Powwow features Native American food, artists, and demonstrations of traditional dance and dress.

Like the state's Native Americans, many of New York's other cultural groups honor and celebrate their own traditions. For example, New York City hosts the world's largest St. Patrick's Day Parade. Many other groups, including Puerto Ricans, Chinese Americans, and Italian Americans, also hold colorful parades and festivals, both in New York City and throughout the state.

The Puerto Rican Day Parade is held every year on the second Sunday in June. The parade honors Puerto Rican immigrants and descendants living in the United States.

The Museum of Modern Art in New York City maintains a rotating display of modern and contemporary art exhibits. The museum features more than 10,000 artists.

Arts and Entertainment

New York is a leading center for the arts. In the 1800s, the Hudson River valley's scenery inspired artists such as Thomas Cole to paint beautiful landscapes of the valley and the Catskill Mountains. Their painting style later became known as the Hudson River School. In the 1940s, artists working, living, or exhibiting in New York City developed a style known as **abstract expressionism**, which dominated Western art during the next decade. In the 1960s, New York–based Andy Warhol and Robert Rauschenberg were leaders in the creation of **pop art**. The state's visual artists continue to be innovators in the art world.

Since the 1890s, Manhattan's Broadway has been among the world's leading theater districts. Stage performers from around the world often dream of performing on Broadway. New York City's Carnegie Hall, which opened in 1891, has hosted many of the world's greatest classical musicians.

The Phantom of the Opera opened in 1988 and is the longest continually-running Broadway show.

The second-largest concert in the world was held in Central Park by the **New York Philharmonic** and was attended by more than 800,000 people.

Many celebrated writers and entertainers have links to the Empire State. Walt Whitman, considered by many to be the nation's greatest poet, was born on Long Island in 1819. Other important New York authors include Herman Melville, who wrote the great whaling adventure *Moby Dick*, and Washington Irving, a popular essayist and short-story writer. Edith Wharton, author of *The Age of Innocence*, was the first woman to receive a Pulitzer Prize. Playwrights from New York include Eugene O'Neill, Arthur Miller, and Neil Simon.

Filmmaker and screenwriter Judd Apatow, comedian Amy Schumer, and singer Jennifer Lopez are all entertainers from New York City. Other New York natives include comedian Tracy Morgan, singer Christina Aguilera, and movie star Scarlett Johansson. Musical superstars Alicia Keys, Jay-Z, and Lady Gaga also have New York roots.

Jay-Z, one of the most successful hip hop artists in the U.S., was born in Brooklyn, New York.

The New York City Ballet has about 90 dancers and is the largest dance company in the United States.

Sports and Recreation

New Yorkers enjoy a variety of outdoor activities. In the warmer months, outdoor enthusiasts flock to the state's mountains and forests to go hiking, camping, or mountain climbing. Boating, fishing, and swimming are popular pastimes at Lake George, the Thousand Islands, and the Finger Lakes. The Hudson River offers canoeing and whitewater rafting, while sailing is a favorite activity off the Atlantic coast. In the winter, New York's snow-covered mountains provide great opportunities for skiing, snowboarding, and tobogganing, and its many wilderness trails are ideal for cross-country skiing and snowmobiling.

The New York Knicks were established in 1946. They have won two championships, one in 1970 and the other in 1973.

On **April 15, 1947**, at **Ebbets Field** in Brooklyn, **Jackie Robinson** became the **first African American** to play in a **Major League Baseball game.**

At the 2008 Grand Prix, at Icahn Stadium in New York, **Usain Bolt** broke the then world record time in the **100-meter dash**.

Professional sports are very popular in New York. The state has three professional National Hockey League teams, the Buffalo Sabres, the New York Rangers, and the New York Islanders. Pro football fans throughout the state cheer for three teams in the National Football League, the Buffalo Bills, the New York Giants, and the New York Jets. The New York Knicks and the Brooklyn Nets play in the National Basketball Association. The New York Liberty compete in the Women's National Basketball Association.

Known throughout the world, the New York Yankees have been the most successful team in Major League Baseball history. Some of baseball's greatest players, including Babe Ruth, Lou Gehrig, Joe DiMaggio, Mickey Mantle, and Derek Jeter have worn the Yankee pinstripes. New York's other Major League Baseball team, the Mets, play their home games at Citi Field in Queens.

Alex Rodriguez, of the New York Yankees, has been named to the All-Star team 14 times and named Most Valuable Player three times.

Lake Placid, New York, which is known for a variety of winter sports, hosted the Winter Olympics in 1932 and again in 1980.

Get To Know
NEW YORK

Oneida, New York, is home to the **world's smallest church**. It is 51 inches wide and 81 inches tall and seats 2 people.

NEW YORK WAS HOST TO THE FIRST AMERICAN CHESS TOURNAMENT, HELD IN 1843.

New York residents may not hang clothes on a **clothesline** without first purchasing a **license**.

The *New York Post* is the **oldest-running newspaper** in the United States. It was started by Alexander Hamilton in 1803.

New York City has **842 miles** of subway track.

One of the world's leading art museums, the **Metropolitan Museum of Art** houses **2 million** art objects.

THE STATUE OF LIBERTY, A GIFT FROM FRANCE, WAS PACKED IN **214** WOODEN CRATES AND SHIPPED TO THE U.S. IN 1885.

Brain Teasers

What have you learned about New York after reading this book? Test your knowledge by answering these questions. All of the information can be found in the text you just read. The answers are provided below for easy reference.

1 What is the capital of New York?

2 In what year did Henry Hudson sail up the river that was later named after him?

3 In what year did the Dutch settle New Amsterdam?

5 Which two main Native American groups inhabited much of New York by the late 1500s?

4 From what continent was the common house sparrow introduced to New York in the 1850s?

6 Which two groups make up New York's largest minorities?

7 Who heads the executive branch of the New York state government?

8 On what date did New York enter the union?

Key Words

abstract expressionism: an artistic style developed in the 1940s that used bold and unusual brush strokes, including paint splattering and solid fields of color

archaeological: having to do with the study of ancient artifacts

Canadian Shield: the extensive region making up much of northern and central Canada, made of rocks that have been eroded to produce a low, shield-like profile

coniferous: types of trees that bear cones and are usually evergreens

deciduous: types of trees that shed their leaves annually

hydroelectric power: electricity generated using the power of moving water

metropolitan area: a large city and its surrounding communities

persecution: harassing or subjecting people to ill-treatment based on their religion, race, place of origin, or beliefs

pharmaceuticals: medicinal drugs

pop art: art movement born in New York City in the 1960s that used images borrowed from popular culture, such as soup cans, comic strips, and road signs

reservations: lands set aside for use by Native Americans

Index

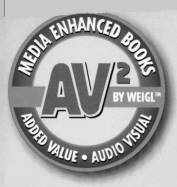

Log on to www.av2books.com

AV² by Weigl brings you media enhanced books that support active learning. Go to www.av2books.com, and enter the special code found on page 2 of this book. You will gain access to enriched and enhanced content that supplements and complements this book. Content includes video, audio, weblinks, quizzes, a slide show, and activities.

AV² Online Navigation

Book Pages
AV² pages directly correspond to pages in the book.

Key Words
Study vocabulary, and complete a matching word activity.

Quizzes
Test your knowledge.

Slide Show
View images and captions, and prepare a presentation.

Audio
Listen to sections of the book read aloud

Video
Watch informative video clips.

Embedded Weblinks
Gain additional information for research.

Try This!
Complete activities and hands-on experiments.

AV² was built to bridge the gap between print and digital. We encourage you to tell us what you like and what you want to see in the future.

Sign up to be an AV² Ambassador at www.av2books.com/ambassador.